9

The Poetry Book Society
Anthology 1988–1989

The
Poetry Book Society
Anthology 1988–1989

Edited with an Introduction by
DAVID CONSTANTINE

Hutchinson
London Sydney Auckland Johannesburg

This edition first published in 1988 by Hutchinson Ltd., an imprint of
Century Hutchinson Ltd., Brookmount House, 62–65 Chandos Place, London
WC2N 4NW, and by the Poetry Book Society Ltd., 21 Earls Court Square,
London SW5

Century Hutchinson Australia (Pty) Ltd.,
89–91 Albion Street, Surry Hills, NSW 2010, Australia

Century Hutchinson New Zealand Ltd.,
PO Box 40-086, 32–34 View Road, Glenfield, Auckland 10

Century Hutchinson South Africa (Pty) Ltd.,
PO Box 337, Bergvlei 2012, South Africa

Phototypeset in Linotron Times
by Rowland Phototypesetting Ltd.,
Bury St Edmunds, Suffolk
Printed and bound in Great Britain by
Anchor Brendon Ltd, Tiptree, Essex

British Library Cataloguing in Publication Data

The Poetry Book Society anthology 1988–1989.
  1. Poetry in English, 1945– – Anthologies
  I. Constantine, David J. (David John)
  1944–   II. Poetry Book Society
  921'.914'08

  ISBN 0-09-173652-8

Contents

Introduction

Nobody, I hope, will think this anthology a definitive demonstration of what British and Irish poetry has been up to in the last twelve months. The compiler's knowledge was not wide enough for that; nor, perhaps, were his tastes. Besides, there are too many accidentals in the job: who was available to be written to, who bothered to write back, who happened to have a poem fit for the world to see. I enjoyed that element of randomness as one might a certain degree of irresponsibility. You send out your begging letters, your doves of hope, your bread upon the waters, your final demands – and wait for Postman Pat. Somebody – it won't be me – might well write a poem about compiling a poetry anthology. This very week – just as I am finishing (giving up, guillotined by a deadline) – one of my eight £1 premium bonds, taken out for me by my favourite aunt it must be thirty years ago, at last comes up, and I get a cheque for £50. I connect that, tenuously perhaps, with happy moments in the previous weeks when I struck lucky and poems came through our door.

Poems, real poems. One way and another I read a lot of verse, much of it not very good. You know the real thing because it surprises you. That surprise is very significant: in it lies proof of the infinite shifting variety of life, and of poetry's agility. Poetry combats stasis, combats the hardening of our postures and perceptions, by being itself agile. I know places where at first sight it is not easy to distinguish between the quick and the dead. Among poems it is, and the quick poem is a powerful illuminator of quickness and deadness in the lives we lead.

I said that this could not be an exhaustive anthology, but it is a very varied one: men and women of different ages, localities, accents, circumstances, commitments, needs and casts of mind. Some already deservedly well known; others, I thought when choosing them, deserving to become well known. The British Isles and the island of Ireland are extraordinarily rich, and the English language, as handled by the men and women here, discovers new expressive possibilities all the time. Surely a reader of this book will be encouraged? I was, putting it together. I felt I was on the radical surviving ground of these islands' culture, where there is resistance and revolt, where a revulsion might come from against the official reign. Here it is being said, it is being insisted upon: there are better lives and there are worse lives, there are ways of living in which more or less of the personality is involved, there is a meaning worth developing in the word 'humankind'.

Some poems here reflect, quite precisely, upon recent events. Some poets have the gift of being obviously topical. The gift others have lies in obliqueness and displacement: you must search out the connection, realize it. But there are virtues besides topicality, there is the 'one story and one story only' (in all its manifold versions) that Robert Graves spoke of. You will certainly find here poems which *happen* to have been written recently and doubtless at some specific instigation, but which are perennial in their concerns and their appeal.

Contemporary verse in English is written in a great variety of forms, registers and tones of voice. I think this anthology illustrates that obvious fact. Sometimes form is a matter of the poem's own making; it is a shape or rhythm peculiar to the poem's immediate needs. Elsewhere what suits best are forms that have been in constant European use for centuries. Many modern poets, more than is often supposed, enjoy rhyme and metre and hark back consciously to traditional accomplishments. And anyone who thinks conventional form bespeaks a conventional thinking and imagination could be cured of that view by reading carefully here. Surprise, as I said earlier, is for many reasons a desirable effect in poetry, and form is a principal means of it, a means by which the force of the novel perception is released. Odd diction is another, language at odds with what is received as standard.

I was very pleased to be told that last year's anthology, compiled by Gillian Clarke, is being used in at least one school as a set text. Contemporary verse, whether it will last or not, has peculiar importance in that it shows what we face today, it shows what might be done, it discovers our truth: the harsh facts we would rather not see and the authentic life we *might* be capable of. In philistine, mercenary and cynical times poetry is a ground and means of opposition. It can persuade you of two things simultaneously: that there is something worth fighting for, and that the fight has not yet been lost.

David Constantine

Acknowledgements

Acknowledgements are due to the editors of the following magazines in which certain of the poems in this anthology were first published:
Agni Review (Boston), *Argo*, *New Statesman*, *New Yorker*, *Oxford Magazine*, *Partisan Review*, *PN Review*, *Stride*, *Words International*; and to BBC Radio 3 and Radio 4 for other poems which have been broadcast.

FLEUR ADCOCK

My Father

When I got up that morning I had no father.
I know that now. I didn't suspect it then.
They drove me through the tangle of Manchester
to the station, and I pointed to a sign:

'Hulme' it said – though all I saw was a rubbled
wasteland, a walled-off dereliction. 'Hulme –
that's where they lived' I said, 'my father's people.
It's nowhere now.' I coughed in the traffic fumes.

Hulme and Medlock. A quarter of a mile
to nowhere, to the names of some nothing streets
beatified in my family history file,
addresses on birth and marriage certificates:

Back Clarence Street, Hulme; King Street (but which one?);
One-in-Four Court, Chorlton-upon-Medlock.
Meanwhile at home on my answering machine
a message from New Zealand: please ring back.

In his day it was factory smoke, not petrol,
that choked the air and wouldn't let him eat
until, the first day out from Liverpool,
sea air and toast unlocked his appetite.

He took up eating then, at the age of ten –
too late to cancel out the malnutrition
of years and generations. A small man,
though a tough one. He'll have needed a small coffin.

I didn't see it; he went to it so suddenly,
too soon, with both his daughters so far away:
a box of ashes in Karori Cemetery,
a waft of smoke in the clean Wellington sky.

Even from here it catches in my throat
as I puzzle over the Manchester street-plan,
checking the index, magnifying the net
of close-meshed streets in M2 and M1.

Not all the city's motorways and high-rise.
There must be roads that I can walk along
and know they walked there, even if their houses
have vanished like the cobble-stones – that throng

of Adcocks, Eggingtons, Joynsons, Lamberts, Listers.
I'll go to look for where they were born and bred.
I'll go next month; we'll both go, I and my sister.
We'll tell him about it, when he stops being dead.

One Way

'I might have thrown poor words away
And been content to live'

*

'We'll learn that sleeping isn't death'
— W. B. Yeats

'One way is it?' (Those words again.) *'Galway?'*
he asked again: was it one way I wanted?
'A single.' Half asleep, I heaved my case
onto the rack, and must have looked as haunted
then as the night before in Donegal
when I imagined, with the moonlit bay
glowing behind the gauze, I saw her face
out in the dark, appearing through a swirl
of cloud, then fading as the soft rain slanted
across the mountain like the spirit of the place.

Nothing touched me. The days just slipped away.
In Drumcliff churchyard I remembered Yeats's
words on death, *Ancient Ireland knew it all*.
My ticket made me think of *Galway Races*,
the disappointed patriot, his life spent
with useless words, whose love would never play
his ideal woman, though as mythical
Cathleen he'd felt the spirit of Ireland
breathe through Maud Gonne's performance, as his phrases
rose from her throat, her voice trembling for the people.

The first time guns were levelled at me
my country's soldiers were responsible.
I watched their revving armoured cars reversed
back down her roads, like one of her people
but also an intruder in their eyes,
unused to what they witnessed every day.

I wondered how she'd let herself be cast
as victim in their rescue exercise
when helicopters on the night patrol
jabbered above, and died away over Belfast.

Their murmur stalked me when I lost my way
one night in a Republican stronghold
where gunmen appeared from every gable
like wraiths, when numbed by unlit fog-filled
streets, numbed beyond shock or sense of danger,
my desolation made a ghost of me;
so drained of hope I was invisible
the other side of a one-way mirror
reflecting nothing but that frozen world
I stared into, a mourner at a funeral,

like when I'd whispered to her as she lay
asleep, as though *I love you* were a spell
to make her want the one who kissed her back
to life, whose arm her own arm wandering fell
across, who watched her coming slowly to
and saw this vigil was as much one way
as a wake, given what she'd give him back:
the hands now hovering, at a quarter to,
their last act the moment her alarm bell
rang, almost touching her face, and holding her back.

Ol Style Freedom

    Darlin mi darlin
you lying down
all legs belly bosom face
quiet-quiet in room here
All of all so much –
street poverty can't touch me now
Hurts – threats – banished away

No pockets on me
  I a millionaire
No test before me to fail me
  I know I know everything

    Darlin mi darlin
you the offerin with all things
  all of all so much
every tick of clock stopped
every traffic groan switched off
every peep of bird shut up
only sea waves risin risin

    Hope she fixed sheself fo no-baby
I in a king time king time king time
  king time
    king time
      king time

JAMES BERRY

New Catalyst

1
An allocated past triggers him.
A category sews him up
in a figure from Mars.
And he attracts obstacles.
He attracts crime labels
like compulsory tags branded
GOVERNMENT. He attracts a house
to be marked and exploded in flames.

A fascination about him excites
moves to hunt and win. Often
he is a whale's experience
looking for a barbed missile.
And his speech impresses as drumming.
Sometimes just his glance makes him
a colourful clown. His presence alone
tickles gentlemen and un-gentlemen alike
to gesture distances of alien oddity.

2
Comes – opens our gate.
Comes, across our grass.
Parched and pinched.
Unripe – yet wrinkled like raisin
smelling of waste and weather
talking gibberish.
Comes and stands at our door.
Wants fruit of a private garden.

Comes – knocks our door.
Two-legged mudhole drinker.
Damned well bred on waste.
Bred on owning all
of that sameness of poverty.
Made in havenots' habits and looks.
Shaped in news that's damned bad news.
And – trampled down boundaries!

Comes and stands.
Nothing inheritor.
Minder of one pot.
Tying of sticks the skills –
wants privilege earned.
And wants to have a castle cracked.

EAVAN BOLAND

Spring at the Edge of the Sonnet

Late March and I'm still lighting fires –

last night's frost which killed the new
shoots of ivy in the terracotta churn
has turned the fields of wheat and winter barley

to icy slates on the hills rising
outside the windows of our living room.

Still, there are signs of change. Soon
the roofs of cars, which last month were
oracles of ice and unthawed dawns

will pass by, veiled in blooms from
the wild plum they parked under overnight.

Last night, driving back from town,
the dark was in and the lovers were
out in doorways, using them as windbreaks,
making shadows seem nothing more than

sweet exchequers for a homeless kiss.

CHARLES CAUSLEY

Forbidden Games

A lifetime, and I see them still:
My aunt, my mother, silently
Held by the stove's unflinching eye
Inside the tall house scaled with slate.
The paper boy runs up the hill,
Cries *'Echo!'* to the black-blown sky.
The tin clock on the kitchen shelf
Taps seven. And I am seven. And lie
Flat on the floor playing a game
Of *Snakes & Ladders* by myself.

Upstairs, my father in his bed,
Shadowed still by the German War,
A thin light burning at his head,
To me is no more than a name
That's also mine. I wonder what
The two women are waiting for.
My aunt puts down her library book.
My mother winds a bit of wool.
Each gives to each a blinded look.
'Your father's with the angels now.'
Which of them speaks I cannot tell.
And then I say to them, 'I know.'
And give the dice another throw.

GILLIAN CLARKE

Neighbours

That spring was late. We watched the sky
and studied charts for shouldering isobars.
Birds were late to pair. Crows drank from the lamb's eye.

Over Finland small birds fell: song thrushes
steering north, smudged signatures on light,
migrating warblers, nightingales.

Wing-beats failed over fjords, each lung a sip of gall.
Children were warned of their dangerous beauty.
Milk was spilt in Poland. Each quarrel

the blowback from some old story,
a mouthful of bitter air from the Ukraine
brought by the wind out of its box of sorrows.

This spring a lamb sips caesium on a Welsh hill.
A child, lifting her face to drink the rain,
takes into her blood the poisoned arrow.

Now we are all neighbourly, each little town
in Europe twinned to Chernobyl, each heart
with the burnt fireman, the child on the Moscow train.

In the democracy of the virus and the toxin
we wait. We watch for spring migrations,
one bird returning with green in its voice.

Glasnost.
Golau glas.*
A first break of blue.

* *golau glas = blue light*

GILLIAN CLARKE

Mother

When the milk-arrow stabs she comes
water-fluent down the long green miles.
Her milk leaks into the sea, blue
blossoming in an opal.

The pup lies patient in his cot of stone.
They meet with cries, caress as people do.
She lies down for his suckling, lifts him
with a flipper from the sea's reach
when the tide fills his throat with salt.

This is the fourteenth day. In two days
no bitch-head will break the brilliance
listening for baby-cries.
Down in the thunder of that other country
the bulls are calling and her uterus is empty.

Alone and hungering in his fallen shawl
he'll nuzzle the Atlantic and be gone.
If that day's still his moult will lie
a gleaming ring on sand
like the noose she slips on the sea.

HILARY DAVIES

Tattoo in the Convict Camp

At ten o'clock when the lights go down
And they know there'll be silence
Unless it's the dread expected, which is not to be
Thought of once between now and morning,
They turn to the little man cross-legged with his spine
Not fitting the wall and plead with him, 'Vlodya! Vlodya!
Show us the circus!' He laughs, and spits;
Touches their shoulders with the tips of his fingers
Before flicking open the buttons and belt and flies:
His bone-lean thighs are caparisoned horses
Leaping through hoops and back again,
Here shimmying up and down pectorals are the monkeys in
       fezes
Buttocks up to the audience and the pink tutus
Of the trapeze ballerinas bobbing right across
That diaphragm. Here are elephants
Docking their foreheads along a neural column:
They roll it like teak round and round their lips
Testing for flavour. And the lions on the biceps
Shake their manes and canines test for size
The head of the ringmaster popping out
Clean as a whistle to take his bow
From the spectators roaring now for the pièce
De résistance: cannon slowly tilting at the sky,
And a shiver going down them as their heads turn
Into the dome of the big top, hoping the shot
May go clear through the canvas and hit the immaculate
       stars.
They sigh 'Vlodya! Vlodya!' as he falls back sweating,
Is applauded and the spent circus animals rubbed down
To avoid the agues of fear and sequestration.
When they huddle back to cages it's twenty degrees below.

The Prisoner of Katyn

'I have no interest now in what goes on outside:
After forty years you build your hell or palace
From the sticks they give you. I have only these
And they determine what manner of house I live in.
It is like this: always early morning,
And there are many pigs about me –
I was taking them to look for acorns in the wood.
I loved my pigs, had given each one a nickname,
Knew where each had a wart or strange knot in the hide
That you could put your thumb in like a fingerprint.
Some had just littered, and there was one of which
I was fondest, a small female, marbled black and gold.
That morning she ran just ahead of me, enjoying
The cool berries: it was the first time she had run free,
And she pushed at the dead leaves, the cold earth,
With her tiny snout. All around us the mists coiled
Like woodnymphs turning the trees to ghosts
With their long embraces; the hogs were centaurs
In an enchanted wood.

                      And then, in ones and twos,
The cries started: through the pale O of the glades
This squealing of a stuck boar coming closer and closer
Till on all sides burst out of the silence running men,
Their mouths round and red as apples as they went down,
My pigs in a welter amongst them screaming and bolting
Into the executioners' rifles. When it was finished,
We heaved them together into the dug earth,
Watched their bodies curl like sticks of incense
In the milky air. Dead leaves were shovelled over
To make it new.

These were the last things that I saw outside;
Through these last windows I count each twig
And chart which way the first man blundered,
I recompose what kind of noise each man made when he
    died.
This is the house I walk in: it is always morning
And I am driving pigs into the spellbound wood.

Fashioned

It's the maid's furniture we lust after now.
Not the veneered Sheraton she coveted
and was bought when she wed but the blond pine
of her backstairs attic washstand, bosomy
chest-of-drawers, blanket box from a sailor father
that pressed her clothes into service on the top
of the carrier's cart, stripped, as she was
in the parkey bedroom to wash with cold
jug and basin we fake afresh, an attar
of blue roses twined in remembrance
her bodice falling in a frill about her waist
the soft pale calf emeried with goose pimples
by frost curtaining the panes with her light breath
while beyond and below loured armoire, escritoire
in timber solid as dark oak naval bottoms.

Her sudsy innocence has become
the furnishing of our dreams as we switch
channels conjuring visions remotely, shuttles
soar us to Glasgow or past the moon
the boxed particles bombard our dinners
to tender. She blew on sticks and paper
humped coals upstairs in a bucket
the antique market displays so polished
she could have seen her face in its brassy sun.
When she married she left, going home
to learn her children to break the ice
in the jug and wash behind their ears.
She shopped for the rich conker of layered
mahogany teaching us there's nothing new
under the all consuming sun. Blued Brits
swopped grain and tin for smooth red kitchenware
and wine. We try to kindle new fire
out of her raked embers. As she took
her bedtime candle up the cottage stairs
the flame bending above the china stick

did she remember the varnished deal
of maidenhood and wonder how they were
managing without her up at the house?

HELEN DUNMORE

On not writing certain poems

You put your hand over mine and whispered
'There he is, laying against the pebbles' –
you wouldn't point for the shadow
stirring the trout off his bed
where he sculled the down-running water,

and the fish lay there, unbruised
by the soft knuckling of the river-bed
or your stare which had found him out.

Last night I seemed to be walking
with something in my hand, earthward, down-
dropping as lead, unburnished –

a plate perhaps or a salver
with nothing on it or offered
but its own shineless composure.

I have it here on my palm, the weight
settled, spreading through bone
until my wrist tips backward, pulled down

as if my arm was laid in a current
of eel-dark water – that thrum
binding the fingers – arrow-like –

HELEN DUNMORE

At Cabourg II

The bathers, where are they? The sea is quite empty,
lapsed from its task of rinsing the white beach.

The promenade has a skein of walkers, four to the mile
like beads threaded on the long Boulevard in front of the
                                                    flowers.

Shutters are all back on the bankers' fantasy houses,
but the air inside is glassy as swimming-pool water,

no-one breathes there or silts it with movement.
Out of the kitchen a take-away steam rises:

the bankers are having sushi in honour of their guests
who are here, briefly, to buy 'an Impressionist picture'.

A boy is buried up to his neck in sand
but the youth leader stops another who pretends to piss on
                                                    him.

The rest draw round, they have got something helpless –
his head laid back on its platter of curls.

With six digging, he's out in a minute.
They oil his body with Ambre Solaire,

two boys lay him across their laps, a third
wipes at his feet then smiles up enchantingly.

Rock Island

(Tennessee)

Deep pools in the stone bed of the river.
A dry pavement between tumbled rocks
and boulders. Jade yellow of flowing water.
The wide valley closed by limestone bluffs.
Soft tones of blue sky and small white clouds.
Bright greenness of new leaves and buds.

The pale fungus, the litter of bark and branches
from fallen, broken trees along the hill.
Confusion of greyness against earth's redness.
I pulled a mushroom, tall and bullet-like
with a gunmetal glint, and turned it over.
The gills looked inky, sooty, dangerous.

Possum or raccoon, the dark-furred creature
that ignored my nearness? It emanated
misery, a concentration of pain
and stillness I could not understand until
I watched those dead back legs slowly dragged
across the field's rough grass into a ditch.

Poppies

A bed of them
looks like a dressing room
backstage after the chorus changed costume,

ruffled heaps
of papery orange petticoats
and slick pink satin bodices.

Every petal's base
is marked with the same
confident black smear as a painted eyelid

and the frill
of jostling purple anthers
sifts a powdery kohl that clogs the lashes

shading watchful glances
from dilating pupils, as though
all the dancers swallowed belladonna.

The pleated velvet star
at the centre of each flower
is the top of a box filled with jet beads.

The hard green buds
are their husband's fists, the silver-
bristled leaves are their admirers' beards.

The Two Teapots

The small teapot to the large teapot,
Stewed as a pond: 'When you last spoke,
Chuckling generously from your girth and glaze,
There were many who listened, who were friends.
Where are they now?'

The large teapot to the small teapot,
Clogged to a trickle: 'Peace, brother.
Your words are still warm and waited-for
By one who will be loved, though alone.
Be contented.'

PHILIP GROSS

The Painter of the Lake

He has appeared here on the shore
as long as anyone remembers
every Sunday afternoon,

a short man, bald,
with misty glasses and a stiff
limp like a war wound,

and a little box of tricks
that folds out to disclose
bright phials and tinctures.

No-one has heard him speak,
though he hums, no particular tune.
He plants his easel and a crowd

begins to gather, shyly:
children, dogs, then half
the village at a little distance.

He slaps a quick grey drench
across the sky. As it weeps
he works his colours in.

Our lake, our two mountains.
He gives them back to us
and what more could we ask?

We love them as they are.
He washes out his brushes
in the lake, which is why

it keeps its blue-green-grey,
year in, year out.
Only today

he has not come. Instead
your Scene-O-Ramic EuroBus
has scattered the goats.

Do you bring news of him?
Is he ill? Oh, if he dies
what will become of us?

PHILIP GROSS

Forgetting England

   'Zyvrosht,'
they said. The woman hewed a slice.
Many shadowy children, aunts and farmhands watched
     him hesitate:
   'Bread?' 'Nja,' she pushed it
to him anyway, 'Zyvrosht!' It had the taste
     of the first bread ever.
   Now she tipped a grey stone jug:
'Oshru.' The sounds trickled through his fingers
     and he said too much
   and made no sense. They shook their heads
kindly and left him alone. He listened to the hush
     of dust in the village square,
   the clatter of sunlight on ochre tiles,
the flash of a boy's voice on the track to where
     quick syllables of glitter
   spelled 'lake' for no-one else to hear.
He named each thing out loud. A scarlet tractor
     far off ticked and ticked,
   iambic, up and down. He watched
the leather-bound hillside patiently unzipped
     in long crumbling lines
   that spoke to him: 'Homewords. Plod.
Or the lea. Soil. Toil.' Even 'God' for the rhyme,
     but 'zipstitch'?
   Did the gulls, smoke rising
in the tractor's wake, really 'clitter'? He twitched
     awake. There, beside
   him, the youngest daughter stood,
all his strangeness writ large in her eyes.
     'You brought me back,'
   he smiled, at a loss, 'I was far away.'
Her eyebrows quirked. 'Watch tractor. See? Trak trak?'
     he mimed the up and down
   of it, 'Zipstitcher? Cut wheat?'
She was backing away, blue eyes darkening to brown.

'Zyvrosht!' he said.
  She sparkled suddenly, and ran, returned
triumphant, all the family with her, and a slice of bread.

MICHAEL HAMBURGER

Song and Silence

Variations on a Theme of Walther Von der Vogelweide
*   (c.1170–1230)*

The doubters say that everything is dead,
And no one living who can make a song.
Let them consider well the common dread,
How all the world grapples with grievous wrong.
When song's day dawns, such verse and song they'll hear
As will make them wonder.
I heard a little bird lament the self-same fear,
Sheltering from thunder:
'I will not sing till the black skies clear.'

I
In megapolitan gardens, on the land
When air was innocent things heard were true:
Wild birds that condescended to a hand,
For sustenance they perched before they flew
Back into strangeness, a brief juncture broken;
And then, wild words, absconded into song
Where they, not feeding hand or mind, belong.

No words remain but tab-words drably spoken
By managers of aviaries, or the air,
To cage, with expert care,
And safeguard from the toxins that can kill
Residual singing birds,
Residual singing words
Which, huddled now in lines too long, are still,
Showing their keepers what their keepers know:
That they have made it so,
A counter-world dependent on their skill.
Here wings are folded, truthful voices low.

II

Midwinter, but because the days are mild
In grey light missel-thrush and robin sing.
We too, whose weather is remembering,
Not only out of season,
Against it if we cannot sing must mutter,
For soon it will be treason
To doubt the soundness of our commondearth
Whose ultima ratio is the death of earth;
Before the reasoners in their money-madness
Choke all the springs of gladness,
With their machines and machinations clutter
Natural song, the human and the wild.

If dying swans break silence, so can we,
If they keep faith, who have no memory
Beyond their inborn need
Of water, air and weed,
The fire in us, now banked with dampening care,
Must feed on that which smothers it, to flare,
Blaze for the sake of brightness,
Though there are those whom no plain fire will sear
Into a sense of rightness;
Nor in our lifetime will the black clouds clear.

III

So in the end we find what in the end
Is privilege beyond all tampering,
An openness of sky
Only at times the swooping aircraft rend,
A place in which to die
As poisoned birds do, but till then take wing,
Impelled to flight by every earthly thing
The tamperers could reach and nullify.

From sickened air, shore of a sea grown foul
Still skies of any colour set us free
In mind at least to follow
Larks into glare or into dusk the owl,
From a dark room the swallow –
Or ghost of each, the mere trajectory
More sure than man-made missile's course can be
That homes to no inhabitable hollow.

Horizon tree-lined, roof-marked, concrete-cliffed,
But in our lowlands large enough for eyes
To rest on or to roam;
As a last garden, clouds the winds will shift,
Light flowers not fed by loam,
Nor labour, when from shorter sleep we rise
To that residual property, the skies
Louder by then, though birdless, but a home.

MICHAEL HAMBURGER

Aging

It is a return, with the luggage lighter,
Some of it lost, though it held the snapshots, notes
But for whose evidence none could be sure
Where he has been, the traveller come home.
Hardly himself, rid of the clutter,
More lithe for that in mind, in limb the heavier
For having dragged belongings yet again
From house to train, station to station,
From train to airport, counter to gate,
From airport to new lodging,
Sleep wrung from strange street noises, on a rented bed.
There's not room in one heart, one head
For the ten times ten thousand things.

Winter light, then, on a field grown barer,
Some of the great trees rotted, some cut to the stump.
Plainsong once more, after polyphony
That clotted, cloyed the ear and died of richness.
Within a single line, the length and depth
Of all past seeing now, past hearing,
Concert of absent voices, instruments;
And in one faint unseasonable breath
Essence of what the winds of many seasons carried
Across the frontiers, shores,
Parallel, solstice, turning of eras, years.

JOHN HARTLEY WILLIAMS

Elegy

Inside the sadness of a man
who has chopped down his last tree
there is an empty place
where the shade fell, & the chairs
& the table, & the missing people
were cool, out of the sunlight.

Curiously, the man is not sad.
He has concentrated upon two main things:
Upon going further, And going wider.
These occupy him like a pair of gloves.
His wife meanwhile
takes care of the darkness, while the visitors listen.

Only those of us who know
what the man was, or could have been,
drink of that sadness in small cups,
seated behind a window. We would like to go.
It is as if they were not our trees, after all.
It is as if we had not been here, even tho we had.

SEAMUS HEANEY

The Ash Plant

He'll never rise again but he is ready.
Entered like a mirror by the morning,
He stares out the big window, wondering,
Not caring if the day is bright or cloudy.

An upstairs outlook on the whole country.
First milk lorries, first smoke, Friesians, trees
In damp opulence above the hedges –
He has it to himself, he is like a sentry

Forgotten and unable to remember
The whys and wherefores of his lofty station,
Wakening relieved yet in position,
Disencumbered as a breaking comber.

As his head goes light with light, his wasting hand
Gropes desperately and finds the phantom limb
Of an ash plant in his grasp, which steadies him.
Now he has found his touch he can stand his ground

Or wield the stick like a silver bough and come
Walking again among us: the quoted judge.
I could have cut a better man out of the hedge!
God might have thought the same, remembering Adam.

STUART HENSON

The Heron

A servant's soul. He said I had a servant's soul
    and he spat in the grate
and left me crying here like the wretch that I am.
So I thought then I should never touch him again
    and I hated myself
and I sobbed for an hour alone in the cold room.
    I'd had enough. I'd go.
Though the roads were crueller than he, I would walk home.
Then he knocked and came in with the bird in his hands.

He was red – with the heat of straw and horses on him.
But the anger was gone, and his face oddly still.
    I was certain at last
I should never be quite alone; something of him
    stuck with me, a splinter;
something he didn't want to give that remained yet.
    I said, It's a heron.
And he said, Yes, it was dead by the stable door
at the foot of the wall, in the snow, in the drain.

Its eye, he said, was deep as a fish's eye, its
    wing's grey was my cloth dress.
And what kind of help was left for us, when the bird
he had watched a week as it stalked the river's length
    could be driven to this,
to a heap of frozen rag flung down from the roof,
with the rods of its legs furred white in ice, where the
    horses breathed, where the pond
it had poached from in spring was snapped tight like a gin?

Sketching on the Underground

But for the slightest movement of his head,
the eyes' flit, lighting and up again –
that and the pen's quick tremors at the pad,
hid in the rocking motion of the train . . .

This is his way – to pay the unposed
moment his attentions, to eschew the vain,
and what the world would call remarkable,
seeking instead the self-possessed.

The woman is too much alone in thought
to be aware of him at all, and she suspects
only the window and her greying hair.
He knows this is the last true test
of art – to break time's fall.

She will be gone in one stop, or the next.

The Tablecloths

She's looking at me like a doctor
sadly looking at a swollen ear.
Don't move.
Her husband's in the garage making cakes,
his solitude a kind of lamentation
for all the people he has never known.
He wears a scarf.
He hears the blackbirds singing.
He said he was a tablecloth. (It's true –
they called him Tablecloth
because his shirt was checked!)
'I said *don't move!*'

I hear the little inn's sheets quietly flapping.
Black shoes of snow-white children tap the street.
At four o'clock their pride and joy
comes home:
she puts a baked lasagne on to heat.
'Are you in love *right now*?
How can you tell?'
Her mother is a painter
painting me.
She's working with the sea waves in her eyes
and two curled shrimps
inviting me to swim.

The little dog is like a bungalow
waiting for her mistress to come home.
She's growing up to find her caring ways
treated with contempt, the little dog
lying on the landing's sun-pink rays.
I feel so cold.
Stuff paper down her shirt!
(. . . the greyness of the sea her mother drowned in
is lapping at our feet like a kitten . . .)
I am a flower.
I am a piece of meat.
She's looking at my face like a mortician.

Voices of Bulgaria

He's found a bear the same size as his mother
and walks about the dayroom holding her.
He calls her Marigold. With velvet ears

he hears the yellow sea below the window
rocking on the sand-bar like a horse
lying on its side, that can't stand up;

or like the parrot that he slept beside:
he wrapped it in a scarf with hearts on it,
to keep it warm, but even then it died . . .

His heavy hand is resting on her dress,
crushing her dumb sleepy whitened roots
beneath the snow, beside the little villa,

where lost mysterious voices of Bulgaria
are heard among the rabbits, quietly singing . . .
He grunts and ties his hair into a knot.

The polystyrene granules Marigold
was holding back so long come pouring down
like gold and jewels: *Marigold, my love!*

Backwater Windowscape

. .
   . .
      . .
      I wake
and gradually
apprehend
how the pre-dawn
after-rain
         drips
in a precisely
modulated
         sequence
from ledge
branch
and pipe

  – slow turning
s p o k e s
of a clock wheel
ticking wrong
  – these notes
alternate
in glistening
alliance

between space

and silence

  – like poetry

  – like music

- like rain

        drops

     (from

no

   where

we

   know)

cycle

       to

       the

       ground

       . .

      . .

     . .

    . .

   . .

 . .

Learning Chinese

Bronze fallen chestnut leaves   dulled by rain
mice overhead suddenly flurry   dumb night again
unwritten letters books closed   screened faces fled
    cold journey to make   a cold bed

LIBBY HOUSTON

Below Mendip

Crags like bones – for them
and for my back the frank heat
bent on strawberries

Dress Rehearsal

One seat on the climb to the bridge, the far side,
the shorn turf, the churned track, the hauled blocks

And the old couple, windcheaters and socks
dazzling as Indian finches in a petshop cage,
stop there, intending a while, smiles poised
for their first overtaker. In emerald, scarlet,
their grandchild kicks the water in the margin
for wishing she dared step the beardy stones.

On the north bank, beneath breast-deep bracken,
a girl who's tricked herself in hard-edged yellow
weaves the fronds like the fairies used to,
or her mother, into frayed half-hearted crowns,
turning some then to nests, the text of some song
passing through her indifferent as the sun.

Downstream among the copper-green beech trunks
a brown-haired woman in ex-service khaki
marshals undecided tears, arms by her ears,
as she wades through the nettles, the line *Shoot me!*
Shoot me now! in her shut mouth, for the brown force
racing off down the half-carved trough.

Upstream is the top and, stretching from sward to sward
oppressive as a lid, the open sky.

MICK IMLAH

Goldilocks

This is a story about the possession of beds.
It begins at the foot of a staircase in Oxford, one midnight,
When (since my flat in the suburbs of London entailed
A fiancée whose claims I did not have the nerve to evict)

I found myself grateful for climbing alone on a spiral
To sleep I could call with assurance exclusively mine,
For there was the name on the oak that the Lodge had
      assigned
Till the morning to me (how everything tends to its place!)

And flushed with the pleasing (if not unexpected) success
Of the paper on 'Systems of Adult-to-Infant Regression'
With which the Young Fireball had earlier baffled his betters
At the Annual Excuse for Genetics to let down its ringlets,

I'd just sniggered slightly (pushing the unlocked door
Of the room where I thought there was nothing of mine to
      protect)
To observe that my theory, so impudent in its address
To the Masters of Foetal Design and their perfect disciples,

Was rubbish – and leant to unfasten the window a notch –
When I suddenly grasped with aversion before I could see it
The fact that the bed in the corner directly behind me
Had somebody in it. A little ginger chap,

Of the sort anthropologists group in the genus of *tramp*,
Was swaddled, as though with an eye to the state of the
      sheets,
With half of his horrible self in the pouch of the bedspread
And half (both his raggled and poisonous trouser-legs) out;

Whose snore, like the rattle of bronchial stones in a bucket,
Resounded the length and the depth and the breadth of the
    problem
Of how to establish in safety a climate conducive
To kicking him out – till at last I could suffer no longer

The sight of his bundle of curls on my pillow, the proof
That even the worst of us look in our sleep like the angels
Except for a few. I closed to within a yard
And woke him, with a curt hurrahing sound.

And he reared in horror, like somebody late for work
Or a debutante subtly apprised of a welcome outstayed,
To demand (not of me, but more of the dreary familiar
Who exercised in its different styles the world's

Habit of persecution, and prodded him now)
Phit time is it? – so you'd think that it made any difference –
So you'd think after all that the berth had a rota attached
And Ginger was wise to some cynical act of encroachment;

But when, with a plausible echo of fatherly firmness,
I answered 'It's bedtime' – he popped out and stood in a
        shiver,
And the released smell of his timid existence swirled
Like bracing coffee between our dissimilar stances.

Was there a dim recollection of tenement stairways
And jam and the Rangers possessed him, and sounded a
        moment
In creaks of remorse? 'Ah'm sorry, son – Ah couldnae tell
They'd hae a wee boy sleepin here – ye know?'

(And I saw what a file of degradations queued
In his brown past, to explain how Jocky there
Could make me out to be innocent and wee:
As if to be wee was not to be dying of drink;

As if to be innocent meant that you still belonged
Where beds were made for one in particular.)
Still, the lifespan of sociable feelings is shortest of all
In the breast of the migrant Clydesider; and soon he relapsed

Into patterns of favourite self-pitying sentiments. 'Son –
Ah'm warse than – Ah cannae, ye know? Ah'm off tae ma
    dandy!
Ah've done a wee josie – aye, wheesh! – it's warse what Ah'm
    gettin –
Aye – warse!' And again the appeal to heredity – 'Son.'

(In the course of his speech, the impostor had gradually
    settled
Back on the bed, and extended as visual aids
His knocked-about knuckles; tattooed with indelible
    foresight
On one set of these was the purple imperative SAVE.)

Now I'm keen for us all to be just as much worse as we want,
In our own time and space – but not, after midnight, in my
    bed:
And to keep his inertia at bay, I went for the parasite,
Scuttling him off with a shout and the push of a boot

That reminded his ribs I suppose of a Maryhill barman's,
Until I had driven him out of the door and his cough
Could be heard to deteriorate under a clock in the landing.
(Och, if he'd known *I* was Scottish! Then I'd have got it.)

*

But of course he came back in the night, when I dreamed I
    was coughing
And he stood by the door in the composite guise of a
    woman –
A mother, a doting landlady, a shadowy wife –
Sleepless as always, relieved nonetheless to have found me,

Or half-relieved – given what I had become;
Saying – 'It's just from the coughing and so on I wondered
If maybe a tramp had got into your bedroom' – and then,
Disappointedly: 'Couldn't you spare a wee thought for your
     dad?'

(I thought I was dreaming again on the train in the morning
To hear at my shoulder, before I had properly settled,
'Excuse me – is this seat taken?' spastically spoken;
But it wasn't our friend that I humoured through Didcot, and
     Reading,

No, but an anoracked spotter of diesels from Sheffield
Whose mind was apparently out in the sidings at Crewe;
Only one more in a world of unwanted connexions,
Who waved like a child when I fled for the toilet at Ealing.)

            *

This is my gloss on the story of Goldilocks. Note:
It uncovers a naked and difficult thought about beds,
Namely, that seldom again will there ever be one
With only you in it; take that however you will.

KATHLEEN JAMIE

The Horse-drawn Sun

We may lie forsaken in the earth's black gut,
but days are still lit, harvests annual,
skies occasionally blue.
So remember. Pay heed.

Our struggle to surface
after thousands of years is, forgive me,
to break up with a nightmare. Apposite
mate for a horse of the light?

Forget it. Were I not sacred
my work would be duller than
turning a threshing mill.
But it's nothing; an honour.

I draw strength from the burden I've hauled
like a Clydesdale through a hundred
closed generations. But what's an age?
a mere night. I sense light

hear exhumation, the plough-share
tearing the earth overhead.
– Go on; blind me. Hear the whinny beneath
the tremor of sun underground. Let us out

to raise a new dawn this dull afternoon.
Let us canter high and look down.
This is the sacred horse drawing the sun.
Let's see what they've lost. What they've become.

Cloudscape

Clouds coming and going, stretching, reclining, opening up
    a space
For a blue spread, a fetch of an almost sea,
    A Mediterranean in the air, and then
There is a hungry, rapacious smoke, there are hidden
    chimneys
    Venting their rage. There cannot be repetitions, surely
    never
The same sky day or night, north or south, sweet or terrible. I
    Need a brush or a Mozart horn, a serene or nearly divine
Impulse, and so there is a God up there
    Not as I thought in childhood sitting on clouds
But more majestic by keeping in balance the air,
    By simply letting be though deep in control
Of this avid air, this breath that pours out stars
    And fixes them as we travel round them. A Claude
Caught the peace, Turner divined almost every
    Mood and gesture, lashed to a mast he watched
This vast display, this ever-extending, unrepetitious act
    Of light and balance or abrupt of altering air
At which I marvel and silence myself to a stare.

JENNY JOSEPH

The Spindle unwinds, winds, unwinds

As over the high passes where snow is dense, the soft air
 tunnels a route, blunting with warmth the sharp edges of
 ice-blocks that have been frozen solid all Winter

so Spring opens roads into the night, riddling the thick
 impenetrable dark with lifting grey as if it were a gauze
 network whose channels once advanced feel their way to
 open spaces, vistas (though within the border of the wood
 you are unseen from the field) making the tract viable;

and so the same, when the year has again crossed over,
 dipping to the diagonal, the beams will become shorter,
 pulling in, broader and blunter, breaking off against the
 wall of the forest, the days – wavelets of a receding tide
 getting shorter and shorter, their reach up the sand feebler
 and feebler until

 long night, the long untouched closed territory of night is
 here again.

JENNY JOSEPH

Trompe l'oeil

(A visit to an old woman sitting at home)

Old woman
Sitting by the fire
Making a lap from spread legs, and the scarfed outline
Of the little old body in the picture books;
Veined hand forcefully on knee to heave you up
From mental dawdlings mulling by the fire
In order to fetch something, to laugh, to make a rough crack,
Tough enough as old boots are to be capacious
For the lumpy foot that can fit none of the shoes
On offer in the shops; –
Stop being busy and practical for a minute,
Turn your head.
I've blown the cover you use for every day.
You can bring out now the small child from the folds
Of the air where you've hidden her about your person.
She is rising through the palimpsest
Of the way you lean and look and scramble up,
As a shadow strengthens at the strengthening sun.
There's still this young fruit, this kernel, this shape in little
From which the tree has grown,
Not child of your womb, or child's child that, separating,
Continued your life elsewhere, but – ghost if you like,
Pattern within the substance, – rings of a tree
Still living in the wood for the eightieth year
To be there too.

You have withdrawn to look for something to show me
Leaving me in the company of a small bright child
Sitting by the fire heaving its cat in its arms.

SYLVIA KANTARIS

Hiëlte

In what language? I didn't recognise it
or why I happened to be standing at the bus stop
when your international coach drew up.
You were reading so intently, shoulders hunched,
your dark hair frosted (I had not expected that).
I thought, 'He wouldn't recognise me now
in these old rags, my laughter-lines grown sad',
and drew back into shadow. The doors slid shut.

What did you see, I wonder, as the coach pulled out?
I saw your knuckles, magnified in close-up,
rapping at the glass as if you wanted what?
Whatever you were mouthing was too late.
I took advantage of the snow to veil my face
and indicate that I'm not really here
or there, and have forgotten languages.
My lips are stiff with words I can't pronounce.

The other people waiting at the stop were shod
entirely sensibly in fur-lined boots, whereas
I hadn't changed out of my gypsy sandals yet,
the winter had come in so fast. (It was reported
on the News that even pairing butterflies
were frozen in mid-flight, wings still outspread.)
Nothing happened at Hiëlte. If I shivered it was
nothing, cold feet, all our summers turned to ice.

Aunt Emily

Squat, dark and sallow, my adopted aunt
who always rinsed her hair in vinegar
to keep its colour true to life as if
she had some reason to preserve herself,
has died innumerable deaths for my sake,
most recently this morning, in her sleep.

We'll never see her like again; she worked
her fingers to the bone. I blame myself,
though she was ancient. Still, it always hurts.
I'm sobbing even as I'm writing this
in readiness to phone and say I can't
turn up to lecture on Proust today (*Time Lost*).

This time I'll bury her in Aldershot.
People understand bereavement, I must
make arrangements for a decent send-off,
travel, choose the hymns, compose an epitaph.
'At Rest' sounds suspect. 'Merciful Release'?
(Sometimes they nose into such niceties.)

Condolences will drop onto the mat
in my absence if I get the details right.
You have to have them at your fingertips,
though in the end what really counts is just
that whiff of vinegar, Aunt Emily says.
She sits four-square, arms folded, catching breath.

GLYN MAXWELL

Cottage in Forest

The captains halt, gasping: they left
good hearts, barbecued, in a glade,
and the ash, green and wishful there
is scuffed by odd infrequent breaths
but gets nowhere. The captains peer
into the cottage, their hands soft
on windowsills, their eyes wide,
and bitter hollows in their mouths.

Then the knock, and then the simmer:
the captains counting the live twigs
on her one table, while her eyes,
white as the spots on deer, avoid
each guess and question. They say please
and she does more. The air gets dimmer,
grainy, doltish, the roof sags
with rain. The captains go to bed

anywhere: in the unbrushed place,
under the table, by the stove,
on the hard floor beside the bed
they keep for her. The rain lets up:
its epilogues alert the wood
to possibilities of peace.
The cottage shudders with the rough
organic problems of men's sleep

and she is gone to the wet glade.
Nowhere to live, nowhere to rest:
all love involving a slow trick,
all light ever prepared to fail:
but there they are, bulls in the dark,
the captains' hearts! – they are not dead,
only walking carbon, only lost
in wet forests of ash and steel.

GLYN MAXWELL

Death in a Mist

Snaps it shut in the night, the man,
and lets it fall and lets it walk:
it's the good book. It's now the talk
of all of us with mouth to move,
stone to throw, violence to prove,
it's a good read. The three-armed fan

bats the air above my head:
in this hot country men are proud
to bleed, and keen to join the crowd
where voices die and resurrect
as shouts. Sapiens stands erect,
and winds his moral from the dead

electrocuted sinner who
he first forgave and kissed and blessed:
it's in the book. In a gnarled west
I saw it, saw a blacker wind
of birds, on every feather pinned
a human coin. The three-man crew

slid a great bolt across that sky
where salmon-tin believing souls
dragged pasty converts from the shoals
of children. It's a bloody good
idea, they said. The three men stood
upon the shore, and by and by

the one man stood. A slow rain starts.
The profiteers open up
the banks, and flood the only cup
there was for us. In steady rain,
the book, its own damp oyster-stain,
flashes up silhouettes of carts:

crooked ones wading in a mist,
unmentionable, in their lives,
hanging their heads in fours and fives,
believing. But they meet the crowd,
books wide open, reading aloud
why death comes now, why feet are kissed.

MEDBH McGUCKIAN

The Cloth Mother

I sat where the women sat, a thrift pink
Farm-wife; the woodland greens of my dress
Suggested a wheatfield crawling with poppies.

The leaves were so stiff, they might have been wired.
The rain was the size of almonds, in the lukewarmth
Richard sang to the small of my back, 'O Promise me'.

We looked well interlocked, I tended the eighteen
Lamps when the sky drained too light a turquoise,
The house seemed to rise in the air and curtsey.

Later, I played I was my own daughter for a year,
I designed a many-pocketed beaded dress for her
So she could sense the spark of her skeleton.

I reshelved her books, old and new, I produced more
Dreams for her than if I had lived in sixty houses,
To make her feel as framed and central as a night

Without a dream. I searched for her full breasts,
Circles within the circles of her clothes, and empty-handed
Gave her my idea of the lowest kiss, not a kiss

Like a kiss, but as if you were really looking
In somebody's eyes. I never get halfway to orange
In my doorless, stepless dreams,

So she must have thought what the unconceived
Catch in my voice meant, how weak the edge
Of my rain-softened hair.

In the next time-band, the day
With her palms up wears a white accent
And nothing but 'Je Reviens'.

MEDBH McGUCKIAN

The Book Room

I know this room so well,
I can't walk through it.

Three deep windows, all south,
Their shapes dark clots on the carpet.

Fruit and daffodil curtains,
With a bit cut out and pinned together.

Flame has passed over the warm house-wall,
Leaving a touch of red in the cheek.

A waistless vase on a small white mat,
Her skirt pulled up over her bodice.

The bluebell petals almost touch, almost polish
The grey that is so kind as you come in,

A boy-like, thin, soprano line of soulless bone
Like a bangle round the hand of the ceiling.

The green sofa shell-shaped, scooped out of stone,
Or a farm set into the earth, a comb

Drawn all the length of the hair.
I know those steps, that folded cloud shade

Is a web of torn sea, a balustrade
Threaded through with sea like thread

Gloves or sand shoes, a letter breaking
The bounds of letters. A sea

That sounds like an island sea,
A rain that is not a winter or an August rain,

A sky that is a whole where light flies
Like a bird. I lie on my right side

And put my hand up to my forehead,
While he looks out of his window,

And I look out of mine.

SEAN O'BRIEN

Dry Sailors

Becalmed at this table next door to a river
No-one these days navigates,
The water-clerks, white suits in pawn,
Have boarded the island of restaurants
To sail theoretical oceans.

The White Star, the Black Star and Ellerman Wilson –
Their funnels behind the back roofs
Of an atlas of cities,
Those Grimshaws of rigging and smoke
In which all the best streets come to nothing –

We know them the way we know Conrad,
Men longing for water but having to read it,
The lifetime of manuscripts found in the bottle.
So often we finish the night
In the glamour of not setting out –

Foam dried at the rim of the glasses
And fog on the cobbles.
But oceans depart at the corner:
We've known it since first we imagined the tides
From their half column-inch in the sports page

Spread out when the kitchen was mopped,
Since we climbed to the landing, as if from up there
We might see what we heard of the sirens
Becoming the distance. Remember the estuary
Turning for home, and the charts we agreed

Would grow dark as the bed fell away . . .
Then the officer takes out his pen and his diary,
His copy of *Within the Tides*,
To write up the extracts his grandson will find:
Which is always the way it begins,

With edifying copperplate,
The figure bent beneath the lamp, and from below
M'Andrew's hymn, a thrum in every surface
With the promise of a storm, while under that
Lie multiplying fathoms,

Their traffic of monsters and hearsay that tells us
Where *Nautilus* breaches the ice-cap,
That Nemo discovers the fiction of Verne
And the coffin of Queequeg
Is found to contain exegesis more precious

Than anything Ishmael could offer,
Who, let us speak frankly,
Must suffer from too much involvement, neglecting
To number the barnacles clamped to the hull
Or to notice the albatross

Sighing its way to the 'distant speck',
Which might after all have been Hudson
Or Franklin or Sinbad or one of a thousand . . .
Or maybe, the hope we're too old to admit,
Just a skiff on the rim of the maelstrom

In which every text will be sunk,
Where as we spin the compass we can see
Beyond the reach of curse and commentary
An ocean quite empty of all but the weather
And us, and the log we shall quickly forget.

BERNARD O'DONOGHUE

Don't Drink the Water

'Tá an lá go breá!' 'You have the Irish well.
An bhfuil souvenirs uait?* Here I have
Souvenirs my own hands made, from shells
Found westward on the Aran beaches,
Not on this island only, but as well
On Inishmeán and Inishmore.'

He led me past his father who was sitting
In the sun, looking with the satisfaction
Of a tourist over the sea. Pieces
Of crooked copper wire (as it were Celtic
Torques, shrunken like toy dogs from the miracles
Displayed in the National Museum)

Were spread on his wiped kitchen oilcloth.
'Would souvenirs be pleasing to your wife
Or to your children? Children often like
Souvenirs.' All I had in my pocket
Smaller than fivers were three golden
English pounds, and I offered them.

'English money is all right too. We change
It for Irish in the Galway banks,
Or at the mobile bank that stops longside
The music pub in Doolin.' Now they're on a shelf
Here in my study, and all I can recall
Is wondering if he learnt by reading Synge.

---

* Line 1: 'It's a fine day!'
  Line 2: 'Would you like some souvenirs?'

BERNARD O'DONOGHUE

Ex Corde

On All Souls Day for every call you made
To the village chapel (each re-entry
Counting technically as another visit),
Some blessed soul sailed to eternal glory
Amid general rejoicing; for God
In his infinite whimsy can't resist
The sight of innocent children shoving
And sniggering in and out the door.
You could save twenty in an afternoon.

Despite misgivings, you would never say
That the procedure seemed a bit easy
Compared to standing in sackcloth and ashes
For three hundred days, or even to thinning
Turnips with sackcloth wound around your knees.
You're not going to change a system which pays off
So liberally, standing you in good stead
With parents, teachers, deity and the grave.
It's not for us to question the Almighty's
Taxing system. His ways are not our ways
(Even if they're suspiciously reminiscent).

SIMON RAE

Jumping in the Lake

One afternoon, when the fashionable
objectors were gathered under the ilex tree,
the Prime Minister was announced.

He was just in time for tea.
Almost immediately, one of the maids
was reported drowning in the lake.

A smartly-suited private secretary
jumped smartly in, expecting, no doubt,
a heroic flood up to his chin,

but found himself standing in about
three foot six of muddy pond water.
The maid in her billowing parachutes

was within easy reach, but obviously safe.
Her hysterics masked laughter,
he suspected, and judging by the hoots

of Bloomsbury merriment from the lawn,
there had never been the slightest danger.
Later in the war, when the cowman went in,

there was no Prime Minister's private secretary,
and no mistake. He knew
the hull-shaped channel to the deepest part,

and slogged on in with a brick
in each jacket pocket and a sack
of horseshoes clutched to his heart.

SIMON RAE

Vulnerabilities

The last night of his leave he stood before
the mirror, naked on the bathroom floor,

and itemized his vulnerabilities.
He watched the gulping targets of his knees,

imagined cock and testicles dispersed
by shrapnel; then numbingly rehearsed

a messmate's disbelieving grin of pain
when tracer bullets scythed away his shin.

Another had his face flayed off by fire;
his batman coughed a night out on the wire.

And then that shell that slithered down the steps
Of Company HQ . . . He swung his hips:

still whole. Even a Blighty could be bought
too dear. He gave his thigh a pat, then thought

how gangrene ran like wildfire up a leg –
how stiff the cripples tottered on their pegs.

He shivered at an echo of the guns.
But better that than join the gas-choked ones,

writhing and mouthing in the cesspit pools
among the limbers and the kicking mules.

How little those who loved him understood.
Nor would he tell them, even if he could,

about this cloaking, intimate distress.
He heard the dinner gong and went to dress.

DEBORAH RANDALL

Houndspeak Forever

Pheasants are truculent in thin birch
Because it is the season of the shoot
And they are soon to be shot. Cartridges everywhere
Like sawn-off crayons that alway draw red.
We cared for birds once and loathed the spouting rifle.
Remember an albino broke cover
Crossed our hearts
His colourless life had to continue
It was a matter of soul.

Birds are small-spirited and so were you eventually.
I like birds better for surviving
In prescribed ways or dying without recourse.
It ends in the sea, Houndspeak
A cauldron of dogs boiling alive
Lifting the lead sky
Slavering rain on our heads.
Holding in the rain was so good
To find warm flesh in wilderness.

Branches breaking from the starting up place
As if birds could be hard and trees hurt.
We walked to Houndspeak, boots thundering, words
        stripped
To nothing when nothing was a pleasure,
You made your blood move twice, an invincible aliveness
That crackled and kindled
Brought lovers out of the air.
The difference is appalling.

Contrasts put a drool on the appetite.
We picked sticks and threw them for each other,
Caught icicles. Early frost
Had got in the living limbs
To still the sap, snap it off.
It shouldn't have been that cold.
You should have told me about death.
Your silence a pack of lies.
We heartily enjoyed the fire we made.

Bones are invested with the same importance.
I have found quite a few where pheasants fell unnoticed.
Nourishing blood found a way home,
Feathers malingered awhile, almost indestructible
Then turned to bracken
Indistinguishable from other growths.
Not so bones,
Bones are albino
The peg on which we hang our singularity.

Everything in nature prepared me for this
But not the shotgun I took to your image.
Simple to take life
But a matter of speculation
How life allows itself to be taken.
I wish you had seen Houndspeak as I saw it this evening
The pink sun given and swallowed
And a moment's repletion.
The difference is appalling.

75

Nightwatchman

Brother nightwatchman I have shared your way,
Black upon black footfall upon the crazily paved street
And eyes and hands full of each other so drunk
The wine to vinegar as we walk without talk on my tongue
And hands feeling for ourselves as only strangers can.

The lock and the alien roof and the fumble for them
Unseemly unhomely things that we build about ourselves
After marriages have broken I still dream of eggs bitter
And raw such as my father slid down his throat at dawn,
Falling from my fingers so much rage still to come,

I don't remember a time in two years when alcohol
Wasn't wailing in my veins, a substitute for tears
Like the grab and grind with a new nightwatchman,
The surprising angle of the apple in your throat
The lotion in your skin, you don't smell like him,

Stairs are unholy alliances, every one and many
Sneaking under the soles of our feet the squeak
Of female philandering as I size the nightwatchman's
        shoulders
Estimate the blades in there and how they shall
Rub for pleasure under my hands two wishbones wondering,

The door is the single hymen I have to admit you
And you ahead owning me and my womb without name
Flicking your beautiful hair gold and white and shampoo
And I live alone, lone as the furthest star that cannot
Be seen, little girl frantically signaling,

Nightwatchman on my carpet you are so naked, and proud
As a pose, I have watched this maleness, I see in the dark
And I know, and I'm tired, tired of the drumskin belly
The random muscle below, a perilous house of cards
Is building in me, my history frail and impersonal,

The neon snakes of your arms nightwatchman
Wind and wind about me and the carpet rolls us up
And the solitary bed is empty our flesh on the floor
In choreography, and a neighbour rapping his fifty-year-old
Indignation, an accompaniment to my game,

I open my four lips for your fingertips and my cunt weeps
As my face won't, and like an angry sponge absorbs you,
All, and when you are sleeping I watch the night,
Small boys sleep off their pleasure, I watch
The night, and wonder at such perfect death.

PETER READING

Etiolation

One day a lone hag gippo arrived and
     camped on the waste ground
which we traversed on our way to the school bus
     every morning.

Cumulus breath puffs rose from a pink-nosed
     rope-tethered skewbald.
Autumn: a frost fern fronded the iced glass
     caravan window
through which I ventured a peep, but I leapt back
     horribly startled
     when the rime cleared and an eye
     glared through the hole at my own.
(Filthy she was, matted hair, withered leg and
     stank of excreta.)

After that, each time we passed it we'd lob a
     rock at the window.
When it was smashed she replaced it with cardboard;
     one of us lit it –
she hobbled round with a pisspot and doused the
     flames with its contents.
Then she gave up and just left it a gaping
     black fenestration
     through which we chucked bits of scrap,
     rubbish, a dog turd, a brick.

     But when she skidaddled, a stain,
     delineating where she'd been,
     etiolated and crushed,
     blighted that place, and remained.

CHRISTOPHER REID

Two Teachers

Jolly Miss Chard
   taught us 'Hangman' –
     her utterly compelling
game of spelling,
   where a simple gallows
     grew on the blackboard

strut by strut
   as we made our mistakes,
     until every stick limb
of the innocent victim
   dangled before us,
     and the final foot

showed he was dead.
   Such hilarious dismay
     greeted the coup de grâce,
that the excited class
   could generally persuade
     nice Miss Chard

to begin again.
   Solemn Mr Talbot
     was in charge of sixth-formers –
all those enormous
   twelve-year-olds –
     but he once stood in

for poor Miss Chard
   when she was off sick.
     He showed us a toy
that he had made as a boy:
   a little square box
     of painted wood

with a glass panel
   set in the top,
      like one of those gizmos
that tend to appear at Christmas,
   in which a silver ball
      wobbles along a runnel

before the player
   loses control
      and it drops to its doom.
Young Talbot's theme
   had been *Pilgrim's Progress*.
      With exquisite care

he had fashioned the route
   from the City of Destruction
      to the Celestial City
with numerous witty
   devices to stand
      for the Wicket Gate,

the Slough of Despond,
   Vanity Fair
      and the whole rigmarole.
The tiddly ball
   completed the journey
      in his wrinkled hand.

CAROL RUMENS

Berlin Weekend

1

Wasn't it called the Rosa
– With a whiff of the kitsch South,
A touch of the cuckoo-clock –
Somewhere in the design?
The shutters, painted black,
Though not for some time,
Stood daintily ajar.
Geraniums bubbled over
On the flaking sills.
But why was the terrace-bar
Permanently closed?
Night after night, the chairs
Leaned their hot foreheads
Against the tables.
Songs and laughter rippled
Across from the other hotels:
Why such silence, afloat
In the city of no bedtimes?

2

We had a last resort
– An inexhaustible
Fridge that shuddered
At its own miracle.
Rows of sleepy bottles
Pointed like little guns:
Whenever we opened it,
They wanted us.
You gave yourself up to a beer:
I sipped a darker liquor,
Oily as plumskins,
And thought of Anna Karenina,
Displaced for love,
And how love pined
For want of place,

Whatever was done behind
A gilded room-number,
With the passion of grand opera.
Could anything happen next?
The sun was going down,
So we let it in,
Small and shy and naked,
And watched the afternoon
Turn pale with marriage.

3
Spreading our wings, we ride
Into our sunset,
Anonymous as exhaust,
Or a chainstore nightie,
Its wishful furbelows
Crushed, abandoned
Under the feather pillow
That won't be mine again.
But the flight of postcards
Keeps pouring after us:
The *borscht*, whose thrilling red
You judge authentic:
The feebler *shashlik*:
A Macedonian head –
Waiter who speaks Russian:
His following eyes, jealous
As mine will become
When, drunk, you call him
Your Brother Slav:
The flatly urban
Subjects you photograph
For sending home:–
A used-car sale,
A hedge of scaffolding,
An entrance to the U-Bahn.
Then the long walk
To the border zone.
The dearth of vegetation.
The unimpressive watch-tower
Anyone could climb.

lean from the platform
Trying to discover
From a gutted tenement
How you used to live,
While you read a guidebook
In one of the mobile toilets
And occasionally groan.

4
Here I should modulate
To a distant key,
Discover the hidden, grey
Sweetness of Unter den Linden,
Or satirize the two
Basilisks who stamp
Around the Gate.
There is, of course, a tour
From Checkpoint Charlie,
Leaving on the hour.
We're in America, nearly;
We're almost free . . .
I, at least, could get
A return ticket,
And dodge the KGB.
I took instead your damp
Persona-non-grata hand.
Like honeymooners,
Swaying East
To watch the dawn break
Over Torremolinos,
Or Muslims slumped
On any dunghill
At the first wail of prayer,
We meditated
On blood and concrete.
It might indeed have been
Simply a wall
– Some usual, useless,
Surly, inner-city
Lump of municipal shit
The young had tried to claim.

I read the slogans,
The painted names.
Now all I remember
Is 'We have smoked here',
The crimson Cyrillic
Rising clear out of all
That artful, artless writing
On our side of it.

LAWRENCE SAIL

Sea Song

Sometimes the seaman can understand
How the whole rocking prism of the storm
Is a function of sickness – raging light and
Ragged rearing water that pours
The dripping length of his telescope, blearing
And blurring the shape of the view with fear.

But this is not the gigantic detail
Of a real storm, with stanchions buckled,
Lights banged out and gear failing –
This is worse, this is loss of luck
Or nerve, the ship racing blindly beneath
A wrecked sky to the black reef.

Understanding cannot recaulk
The deck that is splitting under his feet,
Or bring him safe to his home port –
But, sometimes, still in dreams he reaches
A porthole moon, opens it and
Finds his anchorage, love's dry land.

Topical

This is the wilderness. We recognise it
By the surrounding park. It has no monkeys.
The locusts and the appropriate honey are gone.
Its sunlit contours murder every echo.
All sound is clamped to the head like earphones.

Under the juniper tree, the only hope
Is that of death, with no encouraging angel
To dream of. And never a drop of fatness to fall
Onto the dwellings, the dwellings marooned in the
      wilderness
Where no voice cries, where all the valleys stay level.

The surrounding park does not have any monkeys.
The locusts have no echo. The encouraging angel
Dreams of nothing. Neither honey nor fatness
Are appropriate. Clamped to the head, earphones echo
The exact repetitions of history. This is the wilderness.

Churchyard under Snow

The newer headstones tense against the cold
having no moss to befriend the snow;
and footsteps to them are specific, directed
not for idle search, but to a particular bolster of earth.
Year long widowers right a tipped vase
and shake the Christmas wreath back into greenness.
A thrush cascades snow off a bouncing
high branch and offers its clear song
over the uniform white ground.
The cold makes it so much worse,
indiscriminate in its disregard
for the memory of this one's summer dress
and the angle of that one's cap over his shrewd brow.
We used to hurry them inside from the cutting wind:
now, from that unimaginable weathering
we can only trust their souls do well to fly.

DAVID SCOTT

Locking the Church

It takes two hands to turn the key
of the church door, and on its stiffest days
needs a piece of iron to work it like a capstan.
I know the key's weight in the hand
the day begins and ends with it.
Tonight the sky is wide open
and locking the church is a walk
between the yews and a field of stars.
The moon is the one I have known
on those first nights away from home.
It dodges behind the bell-cote
and then appears as punched putty or a coin.
The key has a nail for the night
behind the snecked front door.
Carrying a tray of waters up to bed
I halt a careful tread to squint
through curtains not quite met
at the church, the moon, and the silver light
cast on the upturned breasts of the parish dead
locked out for the night.

E. J. SCOVELL

The Poplars

By the river the poplars are grouped
Like mountain groups – their forms seem known so,
And their range seems, like mountain ranges,
Dwelt in by a single spirit.

They could not grow but this way.
We think our fathers told us of them
Or we have seen them painted, not
As trees but rock horizons –

                      yet as trees,
With branching fan-spread high from the tall trunk;
Sieves to light, their fine leaves thinned; the mesh
Part dying now, black lightning wild,
And the living branches as subtle, tempered
As marriage in their mutual moving
In breeze or calm or when we call them still.

E. J. SCOVELL

Pupil and Teacher

She turns her face, a little drawn and strained,
So, so attentive as to seem to be
Emptied, unconscious. When I have explained,
What answer comes, what meaning do you see?

She must endure the calling laid on her
Of receptivity – a child not clever,
Tending her cuckoo nestling, her one power –
To take experience to her heart for ever.

Across the room's half-width I see her mind
All dark, all pupil like myopic eyes,
All sluices opened to her lifetime's spate.
What do my words become, carried behind
To those unrejecting reaches, taken as wise,
Taken as truth – dismayed now at the gate?

JO SHAPCOTT

Robert Watches Elizabeth Knitting

. . . it will be found that
DNA mentions nothing but relations . . .
The relata, the end components of the
relationships in the corporeal world, are
perhaps never mentioned.
(Gregory Bateson, *Mind and Nature*)

Knitting is a bore but Elizabeth
nods and smiles and clicks to herself
as though it were more than just useful.
She goes happily about the task,
moving in and out of it without haste,
perfecting tension, cabling, ribs.
She looks forward to the sewing-up
but not too much, knowing how to mesh
the pleasure of the final thing,
all sensuality and wholeness,
with the independent life of every stitch.

Where does it come from, this compulsion
to call her a whole list of things
other than what she is? The string-winder,
the long-fingered, the sitting clock,
the fur-maker and on and on and on.
From shanks by sharp shears to Shape Shoulders
she is what she is, my hank-shifter,
the one who weaves and stitches up wool.

The needles click in a rhythm I can't get at:
part and whole, part and whole;
two heartbeats, a breath, two heartbeats.
Her lips silently move to mark
the four or five last stitches in the line.

Elizabeth's pattern is cut small
and pasted in her diary: a book of days,
a book of stitches; lunch-dates and meetings,
Right Border and Neckband, Left Front.
There is no picture, only the long strings
of phonemes – purls and plains
made unpronounceable by the feminine science
of the knitting pattern. She bows
her head to translate the printed page
into this odd manipulation of sticks and string.

I can't get my mind round knitting.
It starts to have everything
when you come down to it – rhythm,
colour and slow but perceptible change.
The meaning is all in the gaps:
a pattern of holes marked out by woolly colour,
a jumper made of space, division and relations.

Strange to see these youngish hands,
with no puffiness or obvious veins,
repeat the banal and tiny motions
over days over weeks over months.
I ask too much and am too hasty;
this knitting is an exercise in trust.

JO SHAPCOTT

Retia Mirabilia

In the womb the yard-long whale
moves a femur under its fat
and wriggles a vestigial whisker
at memories of life on land.
But this air-breather, the old land-lover,
if driven on shore faces slow death:
its bulk no longer borne by water
bears back in upon itself
and breaks its bones and stops its breath.

And in their ships the whale-men carve
their scrimshaw songs on teeth and ribs:
'Death to the living, long life to the killers,
success to sailors' wives and greasy luck to sailors.'

KEN SMITH

Hungerford Nights

Before you get through this, before
the next page, before you label
the next breath it's over:
the assassin's device has found you.

His knife of a heart has emptied your own.
Then down the rest of the page: blood,
the book thereafter unreadable, plotless,
the tale of a man with a Kalashnikov.

How he soothes and greases it, nights
in the garden shed, a boy with a stick
in the bathroom mirror of his mind.
What he read, wore, saw on the video.

The symbols slip into their metal shoes,
oils groove the mechanism into one
precision milled moment, rapid fire
along the High St and you're dead.

And you're dead. And you're dead.
Himself he had difficulty with.
It ends with sixteen red roses on his coffin,
one for each of them, like any cowboy,

the ashes scattered in an unknown place.

KEN SMITH

Brady at Saddleworth Moor

Out, this is air, abrupt and everywhere,
the light and sky all one blaze of it.
Count them eleven clear hours of wind
over the world's tops into my face –

this old bleached-out moon always adrift
through the bad dreams of the neighbourhood.
In my ten thousand days I count this day:
the moor, all its space and vastness

I hear them say I say. I find nothing
in all four corners of the wind
where stones haven't changed, tumps, gullies
one blue blur of heather and upland grass

where one grave looks much like another.
Think how many years the rain fell I felt
my heart in my chest a fist of sour dust
forming in the acids of my discontent –

but it knows one thought: nothing's forgot
though my vision's bad, my sanity debatable.
I can forget, I can remember, I can be mad,
I will never be as free again, ever.

Nor will anyone be free of me. Count on it.

PAULINE STAINER

Piranesi's Fever

It could have been malaria –
the ricochet of the pulse
along his outflung arm,
grappling-irons
at each cautery-point on the body.

She lay with him between bouts;
pressed to his temple
the lazy estuary of her wrist;
brought him myrrh
on a burning salver.

How lucid they made him,
the specifics against fever:
the magnified footfall of the physician,
the application of cupping-glasses
above the echoing stairwell,

windlass and shaft,
the apparatus of imaginary prisons;
a catwalk slung across the vault
for those who will never take
the drawbridge to the hanging-garden.

None of this he could tell her –
that those he glimpsed
rigging the scaffold
were not fresco-painters,
but inquisitors giddy from blood-letting;

that when he clung to her
it wasn't delirium
but a fleeting humour of the eye –
unspecified torture,
death as an exact science.

Only after each crisis, could he speak
of the sudden lit elision
as she threw back the shutters
and he felt the weight of sunlight
on her unseen breasts.

PAULINE STAINER

Mrs John Dowland

Do they ask after me
the foreign musicians,
when you play the galliard
for two upon one lute?

Cantus high on the fingerboard,
Bassus on the lower frets;
hands changing position
above the rose?

Here there is no perfect measure
for the visitation of the plague –
no resolution
for figures on a ground –

only the memory of how
you brooded over my body;
and the speaking harmony
with which, beyond all music

I would stop your lips.

ANNE STEVENSON

Eros

For Geoffrey Holloway

I call for love
But, help me, who arrives?
This thug with broken nose
And squinty eyes.
'Eros, my bully boy,
Can this be you,
With boxer lips
And patchy wings askew?'

'Madam,' cries Eros,
'Know the brute you see
Is what long over use
Has made of me.
My face that so offends you
Is the sum
Of blows your lust delivered
One by one.

'We slaves who are immortal
Gloss your fate,
And are the archetypes
That you create.
Better my battered visage,
Bruised but hot,
Than love dissolved in loss
Or left to rot.'

GEORGE SZIRTES

Bodies

A brawny driver with enormous hands
is injured in an accident. At night
he shows his scar. His wife looks frail
as she describes the junction and the dark
where it all happened. Her eyes are bright,
dilate with impact, her shadow stark.
She begins to dance beside him where he stands –
immense, protective, vastly out of scale.

It is hard to know just where to place a thing.
A paper tissue blown against
a branch, the sea's seminal calm
shoving and caving. On the long settee
a couple smooches; a blonde-rinsed
girl, the man moustached and military
like a conjuror. They cling
together swaying palm to palm.

Every night a new performance.
Every night a new forging of links.
There's something in it quite methodical
and rather less than modest.
He wonders what the heavy driver thinks,
and what that frailness looks like when undressed,
what insinuations make palms dance
and how such largeness must be magical.

Like broken glass, the sea-spray
splinters, leaves her bodywork, her slap
of brakes. All couples are accidents,
mothers and fathers, bathers on the beach
among the towels in which they wrap
their changing bodies. They will teach
their children modesty. Their flesh is clay
and kneadable. It smells of innocence.

R. S. THOMAS

Looking

I thought I heard a voice
saying to me: 'Don't look
now, but I made them, too.'

What was I here for but
to look? Through knotted fingers,
a prisoner at a grating,

I peered out at the men
at the boardroom tables
with no 'God is love' hanging

on the wallpaper behind them;
at others bent over
their retorts, accomplices

in the escape of the djinn
out of its bottle. I saw
the inventors of the white lie

exporting it to a third world
where truth was in tatters.
I listened to the hands,

expert on the guitar,
tuning the human instrument
until the strings broke.

I saw the dove plucked
of its feathers by too much
fondling at the peace conference,

and beat on the sky for
an explanation. But the voice said:
'I warned you not to look.'

R. S. THOMAS

Brethren

Here I have no neighbours,
unless those furthest off
are closest to me, coloured
brethren, unreasonably
insisting on their palms'
paleness, the identity
of our shadows. I let
my prayers deputise
for my assistance: Tennyson's
fountain irrigating
nothing but the waterless
territory of my conscience.
My immunity in a racked
world is a perquisite
not for enjoyment. Over
my shoulder from immaculate
pools, as I stare down, stare
all those faces behind
bars. The tide changes
with the punctuality
of the guard changing,
waves bayonet-bright, long-
toothed as the salivating dogs are.
I look at my thermometer
at night that promises
the frost's tinsel, that for others
registers the degree below
zero to which hope can fall.

ROBERT WELLS

In the Meadows

A landing-place, stone coping heaved by roots,
Steps down to water, two rustless iron rings:
Finding these, I imagined a river-journey
From the city to a palace outside the walls.

Cattle range in deep grass, trample the shade:
No building more than a barn ever stood here.
But clear in my mind as when I was a boy
The palace's shape and the courtesies it housed.

ROBERT WELLS

Swimmer

Swimming upriver between tree-walled banks
Through hidden reaches scummed with dust and blossom,

I felt the water's plenty, its slow movement:
A largesse I need never cease to give from.